People in My Community/La gente de mi comunidad

Doctor/El médico

Jacqueline Laks Gorman
photographs by/fotografías de Gregg Andersen

Reading consultant/Consultora de lectura: Susan Nations, M.Ed., author/literacy coach/consultant

WEEKLY WR READER®
EARLY LEARNING LIBRARY

Please visit our web site at: www.earlyliteracy.cc
For a free color catalog describing Weekly Reader® Early Learning Library's
list of high-quality books, call 1-877-445-5824 (USA) or 1-800-387-3178 (Canada).
Weekly Reader® Early Learning Library's fax: (414) 336-0164.

Library of Congress Cataloging-in-Publication Data

Gorman, Jacqueline Laks, 1955-
   [Doctor. Spanish & English]
   Doctor = El médico / by Jacqueline Laks Gorman.
      p. cm. — (People in my community = La gente de mi comunidad)
   Summary: Provides an easy-to-read explanation of what a doctor does.
   Includes bibliographical references and index.
   ISBN 0-8368-3308-2 (lib. bdg.)
   ISBN 0-8368-3342-2 (softcover)
   1. Medicine—Juvenile literature. 2. Physicians—Juvenile literature.
[1. Physicians. 2. Occupations. 3. Spanish language materials—Bilingual.]
I. Title: Médico. II. Title.
R690.G6618   2002
610.69'52—dc21
                                         2002066382

This edition first published in 2002 by ˜
Weekly Reader® Early Learning Library
330 West Olive Street, Suite 100
Milwaukee, WI 53212 USA

Copyright © 2002 by Weekly Reader® Early Learning Library

Art direction and page layout: Tammy Gruenewald
Photographer: Gregg Andersen
Editorial assistant: Diane Laska-Swanke
Production: Susan Ashley
Translators: Tatiana Acosta and Guillermo Gutiérrez

Printed in the United States of America

1 2 3 4 5 6 7 8 9 06 05 04 03 02

Note to Educators and Parents

Reading is such an exciting adventure for young children! They are beginning to integrate their oral language skills with written language. To encourage children along the path to early literacy, books must be colorful, engaging, and interesting; they should invite the young reader to explore both the print and the pictures.

People in My Community is a new series designed to help children read about the world around them. In each book young readers will learn interesting facts about some familiar community helpers.

Each book is specially designed to support the young reader in the reading process. The familiar topics are appealing to young children and invite them to read — and re-read — again and again. The full-color photographs and enhanced text further support the student during the reading process.

In addition to serving as wonderful picture books in schools, libraries, homes, and other places where children learn to love reading, these books are specifically intended to be read within an instructional guided reading group. This small group setting allows beginning readers to work with a fluent adult model as they make meaning from the text. After children develop fluency with the text and content, the book can be read independently. Children and adults alike will find these books supportive, engaging, and fun!

Una nota a los educadores y a los padres

¡La lectura es una emocionante aventura para los niños! En esta etapa están comenzando a integrar su manejo del lenguaje oral con el lenguaje escrito. Para fomentar la lectura desde una temprana edad, los libros deben ser vistosos, atractivos e interesantes; deben invitar al joven lector a explorar tanto el texto como las ilustraciones.

La gente de mi comunidad es una nueva serie pensada para ayudar a los niños a conocer el mundo que los rodea. En cada libro, los jóvenes lectores conocerán datos interesantes sobre el trabajo de distintas personas de la comunidad.

Cada libro ha sido especialmente diseñado para facilitar el proceso de lectura. La familiaridad con los temas tratados atrae la atención de los niños y los invita a leer — y releer — una y otra vez. Las fotografías a todo color y el tipo de letra facilitan aún más al estudiante el proceso de lectura.

Además de servir como fantásticos libros ilustrados en la escuela, la biblioteca, el hogar y otros lugares donde los niños aprenden a amar la lectura, estos libros han sido concebidos específicamente para ser leídos en grupos de instrucción guiada. Este contexto de grupos pequeños permite que los niños que se inician en la lectura trabajen con un adulto cuya fluidez les sirve de modelo para comprender el texto. Una vez que se han familiarizado con el texto y el contenido, los niños pueden leer los libros por su cuenta. ¡Tanto niños como adultos encontrarán que estos libros son útiles, entretenidos y divertidos!

— Susan Nations, M.Ed., author, literacy coach,
and consultant in literacy development

The doctor has an important job. The doctor helps people stay healthy.

— — — — — — —

El trabajo de la médica es muy importante. La médica ayuda a la gente a estar saludable.

Some doctors work
in hospitals. Some
doctors work in offices
or clinics.

- - - - - - - -

Algunos médicos
trabajan en hospitales.
Otros trabajan en
consultorios o en
clínicas.

You should visit the doctor once a year for a checkup to see if you are growing the right way.

- - - - - - -

Debes ir al médico una vez al año para hacerte una revisión y ver si todo va bien.

When you visit the doctor, your temperature is taken with a **thermometer**. You get weighed and measured.

- - - - - - -

Cuando vas al médico, te toman la temperatura con un **termómetro**. Te pesan y te miden.

thermometer/
termómetro

11

The doctor checks to see if your heart is healthy. He listens to your heart with a **stethoscope**.

- - - - - - - -

El médico se asegura de que tu corazón está bien. Para escuchar los latidos, usa un **estetoscopio**.

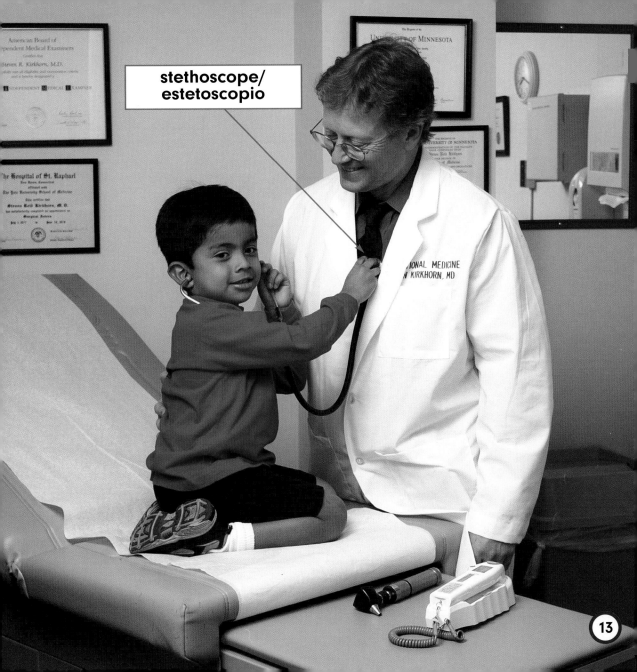

stethoscope/
estetoscopio

13

The doctor checks inside your ears, nose, and throat with an **otoscope**. Sometimes this tickles!

- - - - - - -

La médica te revisa los oídos, la nariz y la garganta con un **otoscopio**. ¡A veces da cosquillas!

otoscope/otoscopio

Sometimes the doctor gives you a shot. This might hurt a little, but it helps you stay healthy.

A veces el médico te pone una inyección. Eso puede doler un poco, pero te ayuda a estar saludable.

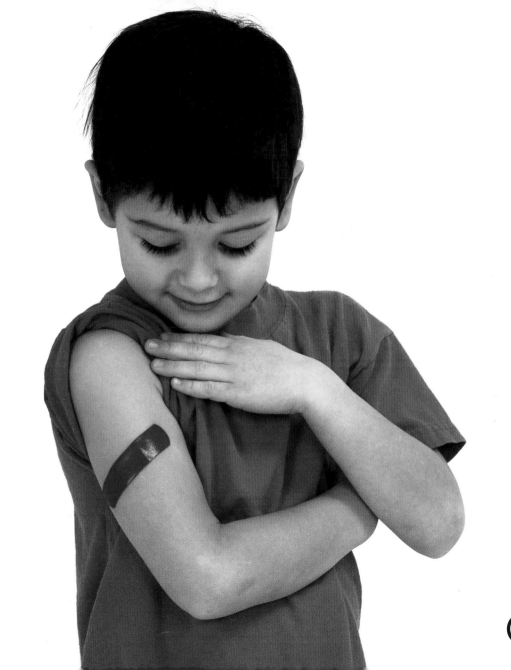

Sometimes it's scary to visit the doctor, but the doctor is nice. He tells you how to stay healthy.

A veces da miedo ir al médico, pero él es simpático. Te dice qué debes hacer para mantenerte saludable.

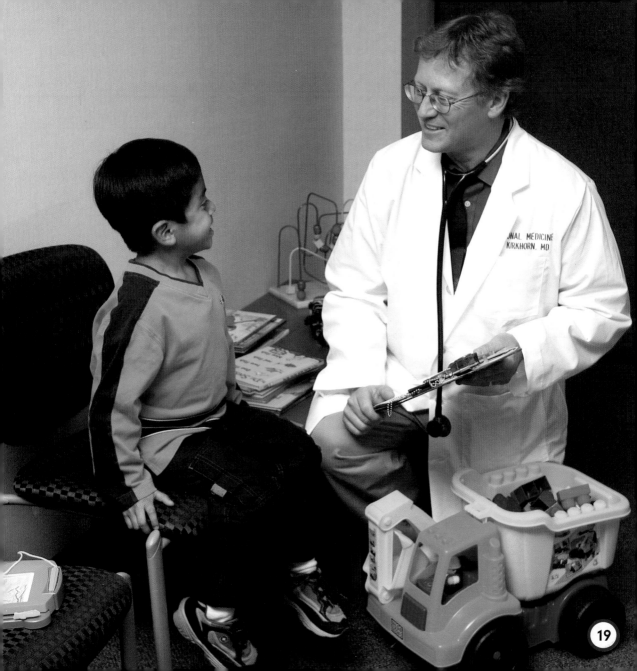

It looks like fun to be a doctor. Would you like to be a doctor some day?

— — — — — — — —

Ser médico parece divertido. ¿Te gustaría ser médico algún día?

Glossary/Glosario

checkup — an examination by a doctor to see if someone is healthy

revisión — examen que hace el médico para ver si alguien tiene buena salud

clinics — places people go to see doctors

clínicas — lugares a los que la gente va para ver a los médicos

hospitals — places people go when they are hurt or very sick

hospitales — lugares a los que va la gente cuando ha tenido un accidente o está muy enferma

otoscope — a tool with a light that doctors use to see inside

otoscopio — instrumento que usan los médicos para ver por dentro

For More Information/Más información

Fiction Books/Libros de ficción

Berenstain, Stan and Jan. *The Berenstain Bears Go to the Doctor.* New York: Random House, 1981.

Davison, Martine. *Robby Visits the Doctor.* New York: Random House, 1992.

Gold, Becky. *Phil and Lil Go to the Doctor.* New York: Scholastic, 2001.

Nonfiction Books/Libros de no ficción

Kottke, Jan. *A Day with a Doctor.* New York: Children's Press, 2000.

Moses, Amy. *Doctors Help People.* Plymouth, Minn.: Child's World, 1997.

Web Sites/Páginas Web

Going to the Doctor

www.kidshealth.org/kid/feel_better/people/going_to_dr.html

What happens at the doctor's office

Index/Índice

checkup, 8
revisión

clinics, 6
clínicas

examination, 10,
   12, 14
examen

heart, 12
corazón

hospitals, 6
hospitales

otoscope, 14, 15
otoscopio

shot, 16
inyección

stethoscope, 12, 13
estetoscopio

temperature, 10
temperatura

thermometer, 10, 11
termómetro

tools, 10, 12, 14
instrumental

visiting the doctor,
   8, 10, 18
visita al médico

work of the doctor,
   4, 6, 10, 12, 14,
   16, 18
trabajo del
   médico

About the Author/Información sobre la autora

Jacqueline Laks Gorman is a writer and editor. She grew up in New York City and began her career working on encyclopedias and other reference books. Since then, she has worked on many different kinds of books. She lives with her husband and children, Colin and Caitlin, in DeKalb, Illinois.

Jacqueline Laks Gorman es escritora y editora. Creció en Nueva York, y se inició en su profesión editando enciclopedias y otros libros de consulta. Desde entonces ha trabajado en muchos tipos de libros. Vive con su esposo y sus hijos, Colin y Caitlin, en DeKalb, Illinois.